WORRIED
about
school
your family
your future
ever felt like
NO ONE CARES

Have you ever ha… you ever worried about school, your family, or your future? Have you ever had a fight with a friend or a parent? Have you ever felt sad because of something or someone you lost? Have you ever felt like no one in the world cares about you? If you said yes to any of these questions, this course is for *you*.

Welcome!

Remarkably, every single person you know has felt these things at some time in his or her life. And every person you know will feel these things again. Somehow people manage to deal with it all and move on.

Dealing with Tough Times is a course about managing life's struggles. You will work with your teacher and the other young people in your group to understand why some of these things happen, decide what you can do about them, and come up with positive strategies for surviving and growing from these experiences.

Everyone struggles, just like you do. But everyone also has times of fun and happiness and pure joy—just like you do. Together the joys and struggles make up this thing we call life. Thankfully we're not in this alone. We have one another, we have our inner strength, and we have God walking beside us every step of the way.

everyone struggles
we have
one another
we have
our inner strength
and
we have God
walking beside us every step of the way

I'm Worried

Here is a list of worries commonly experienced by people your age. Put a check mark in the column that represents how often each of these worries concerns you. Skip the worries that do not apply to your life.

I almost never worry . . .

I worry once in a while . . .

I worry a lot . . .

1. about what others think of me
2. about how I look
3. that my parents might get a divorce
4. about getting a good job when I am older
5. about all the fights in my family
6. about all the people in the world who die from starvation or violence
7. that I might die soon
8. about my mom or dad dying
9. about whether I am doing well in school and whether my grades are okay
10. about whether others think the same things about sex as I do

I almost never worry . . .

I worry once in a while . . .

I worry a lot . . .

11. about what high school will be like
12. about all the drugs and drinking around me
13. about whether I will make enough money to buy the things I want
14. that I might be sexually or physically abused
15. about being the best at something someday
16. about my mom's or dad's heavy drinking
17. about my interest in the other sex
18. about getting beaten up
19. about making friends
20. because I do not get along with my sisters and brothers
21. that my grandparents might die or have to go to a nursing home

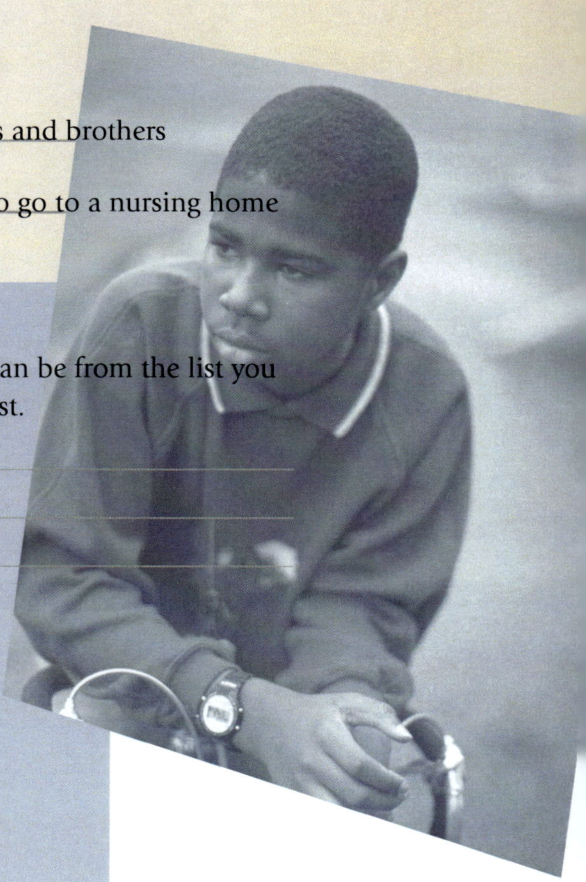

Write on the lines below your top three worries right now. They can be from the list you just completed, or you may identify worries that are not on the list.

1. 7
2. 8
3. 21

Trust the past to God's mercy.
Trust the present to God's love.
Trust the future to God's providence.
(Anonymous)

I'm Coping

Inside this life raft, list the pressures that you feel inside yourself right now. Around the outside of the raft, list the pressures that are coming from other people in your life right now.

When your teacher tells you to do so, put an *X* through the pressures that you cannot do anything about. Draw a circle around the pressures that you think you can work on.

REMEMBER *These Things*

- Most people enjoy life most of the time.
- Everyone worries sometimes. Everyone is afraid sometimes. Everyone feels pressure sometimes. Every one of your friends and every adult you know feels these things. It's part of life.
- It helps to know what pressures you can do something about and what pressures are beyond your control.
- It's important to have positive ways to deal with the stresses and pressures in your life.
- God is with you always—during the good times and the tough times.

"Therefore I tell you, do not worry about your life, what you will eat or what you will drink, or about your body, what you will wear. . . . can any of you by worrying add a single hour to your span of life? . . . Consider the lilies of the field, how they grow; they neither toil nor spin, yet I tell you, even Solomon in all his glory was not clothed like one of these." (Matthew 6:25–29, NRSV)

Psalm 23

God, you are my shepherd;
I shall not want for anything.
In green pastures you give me a place to rest.
Beside cool waters you lead me;
you refresh my soul.
You guide me in the right paths
for your name's sake.
Even though I walk in the dark valley,
I am not afraid;
for you are at my side.
Your rod and your staff give me courage.
You spread the table before me
in the sight of my enemies.
You anoint my head with oil.
My cup is overflowing.
Only goodness and kindness follow me
all the days of my life;
and I will make my life with you
for years to come.

(Adapted)

God,

i know you're there,
always watching,
with me, in me.
the knowledge of this strengthens me.
i am not afraid.

(Hue Hoang, New York, New York)

How Do I Spell Success?

Complete these sentences.

1. When I hear the word *success,* the person I think of is

2. I think of this person because

3. The last time I was a success at something was

I personally measure success in terms of the contributions an individual makes to her or his fellow human beings. (Margaret Mead)

Winning and Losing

Read these brief situations and decide if the characters are winners or losers and if they are successful or not. Write your responses in the spaces provided.

1. Rob is an average student, but lately he has had a hard time with math. He does not seem to understand the material. He has been warned that if he does not pass math, he cannot be in the school play. His friend Kate is really good at math, and she wants Rob to be in the play. One day his class has a big test. Just before the test begins, Kate tells Rob that she will write big and leave her paper uncovered so that Rob can copy the answers. Rob decides not to cheat, and he fails the test.

   Does Rob win or lose?

   Win ______________________________

   Is Rob a success?

   No ______________________________

2. Jill is a swimmer with a local team. Every year the top five swimmers from each team in the region compete to see who will represent the region in the state finals. Jill has never made it to the state competition, even though her coaches keep telling her that she has enough talent to win it in her age-group. This year Jill decides to try to go to state. For a month she works extra hard, and she makes the regional team. Everyone, including Jill, has high hopes as Jill prepares for the state finals. Nevertheless, when she competes in the state meet, she comes in last, far behind the nearest competitor.

   Does Jill win or lose?

   ____

   Is Jill a success?

   ____

3. Chad's soccer team is playing against a tough opponent. These two teams are tied for first place in their division. Before the game Chad and his teammates get together and make a pact to win at any cost. During the game his teammates foul when the referee is not looking. They trip people on the other team, and they try to bully their opponents. Chad's team wins 6–4.

   Does Chad's team win or lose?

   ____

   Is Chad's team a success?

   ____

4. Cindy likes baby-sitting for the Finleys. She knows that they trust her and often count on her to take good care of their little boy and their newborn girl. The Finleys say that they used to worry about leaving a newborn with a baby-sitter, until they met Cindy, who is very good and dependable.

One day Cindy's friends Dara and Janelle ask her to go to the movies. Cindy knows that this is her chance to introduce Dara and Janelle to her brother and his friends. The girls have been waiting a long time for this opportunity.

But then Cindy remembers that she has promised to baby-sit at the Finleys. So she calls Dara, who gets mad at her. Dara tells her that other people could easily baby-sit in her place. When Cindy refuses to cancel her baby-sitting agreement with the Finleys, Dara says that she can forget about being friends anymore. To make matters worse, Dara says that she will tell the other girls and that by Monday morning Cindy will be the school outcast.

   Does Cindy win or lose? Win

   ____

   Is Cindy a success? No ye

   ____

REMEMBER *These Things*

- Competition is a reality of life. It can be destructive and harmful when it leads us to do things we know are wrong or to act in a way that hurts others, or when its goal is simply the accumulation of material goods.
- Competition is valuable when it makes us work to be our best self. The only person we need to compete with is the person we were yesterday. If we can say that we did something a little better today than we did yesterday, we have taken a step toward reaching our goal. We have experienced success.
- When we face a competitive challenge, we must ask ourselves two questions. The first is, Do I want to do this only to be better than someone else? The second is, Is this going to make me a better person than I was yesterday?

God,

Even though I'm not the best at sports, or the best student, you still love me and take care of me. I might not be the best dressed or the best looking, but you created me in your image, and you love me. I might not be popular, but I try my best to be a good, caring, helpful Christian. And you love me just the way I am. That's all that matters.

Amen.

(Christine Mueller,
Severna Park,
Maryland)

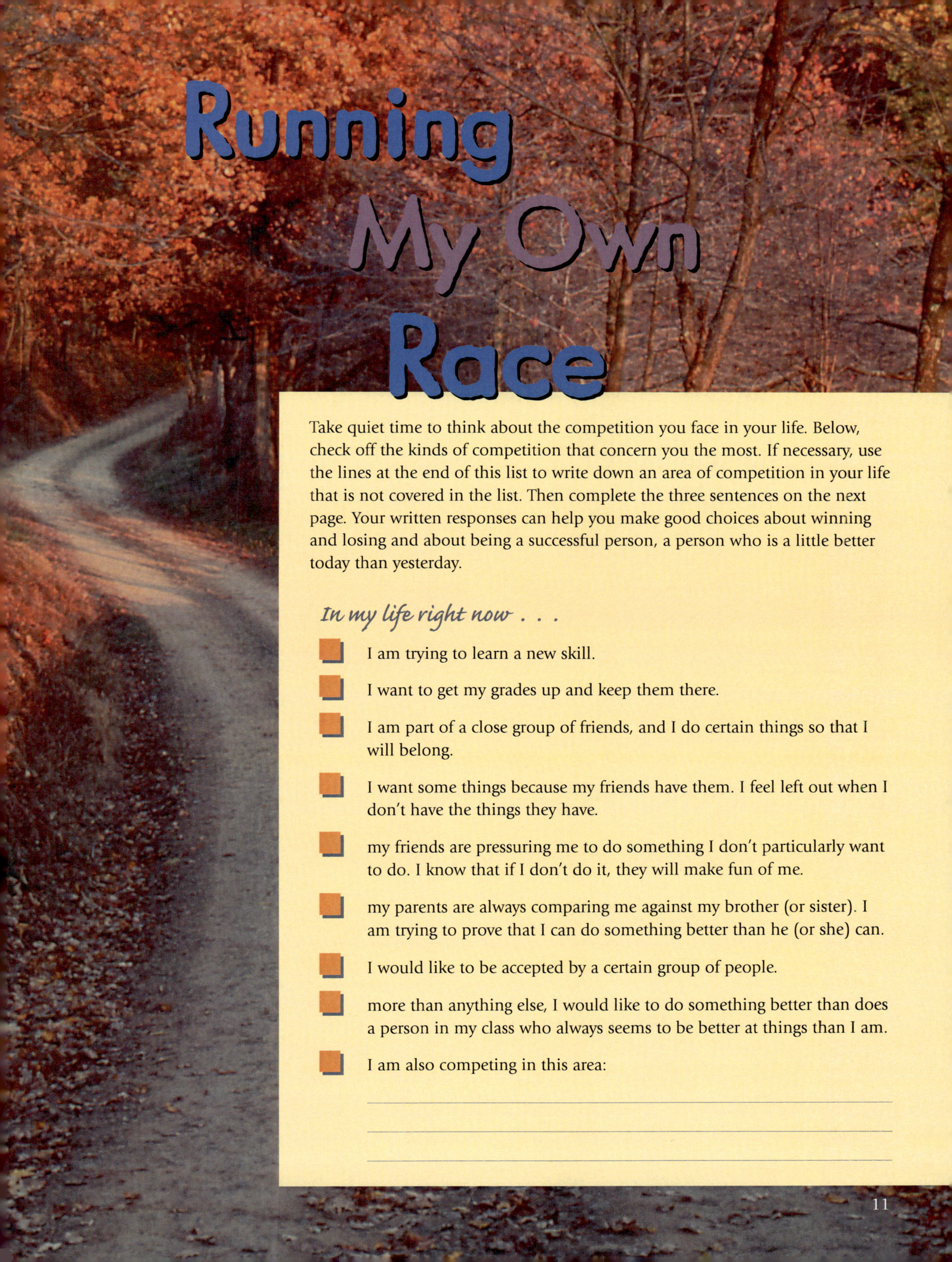

Running My Own Race

Take quiet time to think about the competition you face in your life. Below, check off the kinds of competition that concern you the most. If necessary, use the lines at the end of this list to write down an area of competition in your life that is not covered in the list. Then complete the three sentences on the next page. Your written responses can help you make good choices about winning and losing and about being a successful person, a person who is a little better today than yesterday.

In my life right now . . .

- [ ] I am trying to learn a new skill.
- [ ] I want to get my grades up and keep them there.
- [ ] I am part of a close group of friends, and I do certain things so that I will belong.
- [ ] I want some things because my friends have them. I feel left out when I don't have the things they have.
- [ ] my friends are pressuring me to do something I don't particularly want to do. I know that if I don't do it, they will make fun of me.
- [ ] my parents are always comparing me against my brother (or sister). I am trying to prove that I can do something better than he (or she) can.
- [ ] I would like to be accepted by a certain group of people.
- [ ] more than anything else, I would like to do something better than does a person in my class who always seems to be better at things than I am.
- [ ] I am also competing in this area:

1. One race that I am running for the right reason is

2. One race that I am running for the wrong reason is

3. One race that I really need God's help on right now is

The Race to Heaven

I am still pursuing my goal in the attempt to take hold of the prize for which Christ Jesus took hold of me. Sisters and brothers, I do not believe I have gotten there yet. I can only say this: forgetting everything that is behind me and straining forward to what lies ahead, I am racing toward the finish line to win the prize of God's heavenly call in Christ Jesus. This is the way in which all of us who are mature should be thinking. If you have a different attitude, God will let you know in some way. Meanwhile let us hold on to what we have accomplished and keep moving forward toward our heavenly goal. (Adapted from Philippians 3:12–14)

Failure is an event, not a person. (William D. Brown)

To tend, unfailingly, unflinchingly, towards a goal, is the secret of success. (Anna Pavlova)

Being defeated is often a temporary condition. Giving up is what makes it permanent. (Marilyn vos Savant)

Sometimes I Get So ANGRY

Think about areas of conflict in your life and complete the following sentence-starters. If any do not apply to your life, feel free to skip them.

1. The last time I had an argument with my parents, it was about

2. The last time I had a fight with a brother or a sister, it was because

3. The last time I had a fight with a friend, it was about

4. The last time I defended the group I hang around with and got in an argument about it was when

5. The last time I disagreed with someone in authority (like the principal, a teacher, or a coach), it was because

6. When I fight or argue with someone, I usually end up feeling

Dear God,

I know I may fight with my brother, but I still love him. I know I yell at my sister and my parents, but I love them, too. I just get so stressed out that I take out my anger on anybody around me. Please, dear God, help me to control my anger.

(Caitlin Tones, Iowa City, Iowa)

My Style

For each situation circle the letter that represents your first reaction.

1. It is Friday night. As usual your friends want to hang out at the mall and get a pizza. You are tired of doing the same old thing all the time, but you really like being with your friends. You . . .

a. tell them that they are boring and that unless they do something a little more interesting, you are not going.
b. go along with them because you like being with your friends, even though you are bored.
c. plan to get your friends to make a list of all the possible things they could do together on Friday nights, decide which ones interest everybody, and do one each Friday night.
d. suggest something new to do this Friday night and ask someone else to think up something for next Friday night.

2. Your younger brother borrowed your bike without asking. This is not the first time he has done this. You . . .

a. yell at him and threaten him within an inch of his life.
b. ask him why he likes using your bike better than using his own. If he has a good reason, you tell him that he can borrow your bike if he asks first.
c. don't say anything to him but tell your parents.
d. help him get his bike in good shape.

3. Your dad wants you to help him work in the yard and clean out the garage this Saturday. You have made plans with your friends, and you are looking forward to spending the day with them. You . . .

a. say nothing about your plans to your dad and tell your friends that your dad wants you to stay home. Then you give your dad the silent treatment.
b. tell your dad about your plans. Then you ask him if you can help him out on another day so that you can go with your friends.
c. tell your dad about your plans. Then you ask him if you can go with your friends in the morning and help him in the afternoon.
d. blow up at your dad.

4. A friend said something that really embarrassed you in front of a group of people at school. You . . .

   a. tell your friend that you did not like what happened and that you were embarrassed.
   b. look for a chance to do the same thing to your friend.
   c. talk to another friend about how upset you are with the person who embarrassed you.
   d. ask someone to tell your friend how upset you are.

5. Your teacher has assigned you and two of your classmates to work on a science project that is due in three weeks. All three of you must do the project together, and one grade will be given. One person in your group is not doing her share of the work. You . . .

   a. try to do her work in addition to your own because you don't want to risk getting a bad grade.
   b. have a talk with her and the other person in your group. Together the three of you make a plan that works for everyone involved.
   c. blame her for not doing her part. You make sure that she knows you think she is dumb and lazy and that the project is behind schedule because of her.
   d. have a talk with her and offer to help her complete some of her assignment, but ask her to do the rest.

6. A friend has been ignoring you lately. She has been hanging around with a different group of girls and doing things that you don't like. When you try to talk to her at school, she brushes you off. You . . .

   a. try to talk with her outside of school. You tell her how concerned you are about the things that she has been doing with her new friends.
   b. hang around with her and her new group of friends once in a while.
   c. find a new group of friends.
   d. cuss her out and talk about her behind her back.

7. For about a year, you have been baby-sitting and doing odd jobs for a family. When you started, they agreed to pay you three dollars an hour. Lately they have been paying you less. You . . .

a. try to find a job that pays well and refuse to work for this family as often.
b. keep on working for them, no matter what they pay you. After all, something is better than nothing.
c. talk to them about the problem. Perhaps you can come up with a solution that is good for you and the family.
d. quit working for them altogether. If anyone asks, you tell them how unfair the family was to you.

8. You are on a committee to plan an end-of-the-school-year party. You have some good ideas that are different from everyone else's. You are convinced that everyone would have a great time if the committee used your ideas. You . . .

a. try to get at least one or two of your ideas worked into the final plan.
b. disagree with the others' ideas, but do not argue because you are outnumbered.
c. quit the committee and plan your own party for the same time.
d. present your ideas to the group, listen to everybody's ideas, and try to come up with a plan that will be the most fun for everybody.

9. Your group of friends doesn't get along with another group in your grade. You know that one of these days, a fight will break out between the two. You . . .

a. get ready to join in the fight when it happens.
b. try to talk to some of the people in the other group and think about becoming friends with them.
c. pretend that there is no problem.
d. encourage your group to talk to the other group.

10. Your teacher has asked for suggestions on how to spend the money your class made on a recent bike-a-thon. Your best friend has a good idea, but so do others. In fact, you like a few of your classmates' ideas better than you like your best friend's idea. When it comes to the final vote, you . . .

a. vote for your friend's idea just to make him happy.
b. vote for the idea you want, and explain to your friend why you did.
c. don't vote.
d. vote for the idea you want and then make sure your friend overhears you say to someone else that you didn't like any other ideas.

This chart can help you find your style of conflict resolution. Next to each number, circle the letter you chose on pages 16 to 18. Count the number of circled letters in each column and write the total in the blank at the bottom. Your highest score indicates the way you most often deal with conflict. If two or three totals are the same or if all four totals are close, you use a variety of styles.

	Response			
Situation	Avoid	Work Against	Work Together	Meet Halfway
1	b	a	c	d
2	c	a	d	b
3	a	d	b	c
4	c	b	a	d
5	a	c	b	d
6	c	d	a	b
7	b	d	c	a
8	b	c	d	a
9	c	a	d	b
10	a	d	b	c
Total				

I Can Manage

These explanations can help you understand and identify various conflict-management styles.

Avoid

(It's no problem.)

Some people do not like to argue or fight. They even physically move away from disagreements. Or if a disagreement is right in front of their nose, they act as if it does not exist.

Sometimes people must avoid conflicts—for example, when they judge that the time is not right or that they need someone else to help solve the problem or that the problem just is not worth fighting about.

However, avoiding disagreements at any cost means always losing. Avoiders never even try to get what they really want. When avoiders always lose, someone else always wins.

Work Against

(Wanna fight about it?)

Some people always choose fighting as their first option. They physically move toward disagreements and focus on winning at the expense of another.

Sometimes competition is the appropriate way to settle a disagreement. For example, a sports competition is the best way to settle a disagreement about which team is better.

A fight or an argument is a competition where one person or group tries to overpower another. When this kind of conflict resolution occurs, someone always wins and someone always loses.

Work Together

(Let's each contribute something.)

Working together is probably the best way to handle most conflicts because both sides win. Everybody is satisfied with the solution, because everyone has given something and everyone has received something.

Meet Halfway

(You win some; you lose some.)

Meeting halfway can be good sometimes because both sides end up winning something, but they end up losing something too. This is a fair way of dealing with choices that people have to make together. It works best when everybody realizes that both sides will lose something.

Summary

These four ways of dealing with disagreements are all useful and even necessary some of the time. In facing a conflict, first decide if the situation calls for a clear winner or loser. Most conflicts do not call for a winner or a loser; most call for winners. When that is the case, work to resolve the conflict so that everybody wins. Remember that nobody likes to lose.

REMEMBER *These Things*

- Conflict is inevitable. How you handle conflict is your choice.
- The easy way out is not always the best way. It may be easy to walk away from a conflict or to be aggressive and fight, but in either case someone will end up losing and getting hurt.
- Apologize to people you hurt. Forgive those who hurt you.
- Be kind—every single moment of your life.

The world is wide, and I will not waste my life in friction when it could be turned into momentum. (Frances Willard)

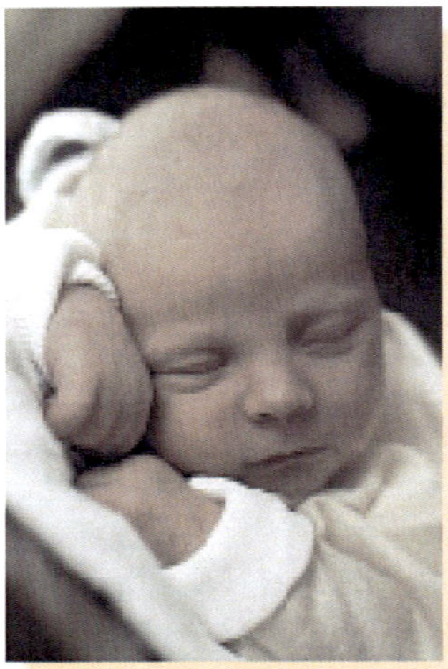

Somewhere Along the Way

This time line represents your life from birth to the present. Read the list of events on page 23 and write on the time line the letter of each event that you have experienced. If an important loss in your life is not listed, write it on one of the blank lines at the end of the list and put its letter on the time line. Each letter may be used more than once.

Birth

I Dont Know

Age 5

a

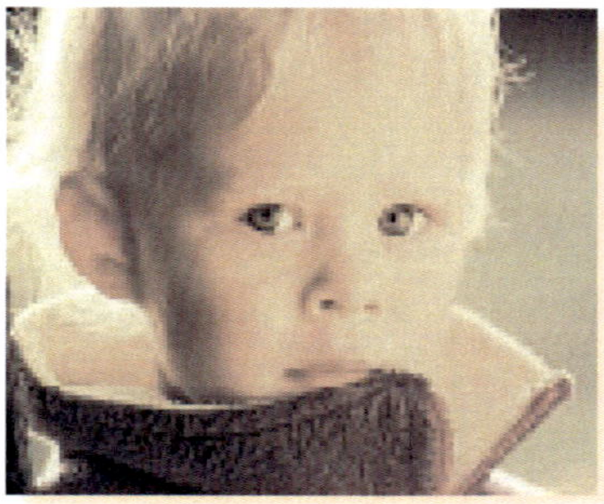

Losing is the price we pay for living. It is also the source of much of our growth and gain. (Judith Viorst)

Events

a. I stopped believing in Santa Claus.
b. I lost a favorite toy.
c. I moved to a new school.
d. My team lost a big game.
e. A brother or a sister left home.
f. A close friend moved.
g. I had a fight that ended a friendship.
h. I lost a pet.
i. I learned that my parents were separating.
j. I got grounded for breaking a rule at home.

k. I got cut from a team.
l. I got rejected by a member of the other sex.
m. My family moved.
n. My grades went down.
o. Someone close to me died.
p. I became sick enough to be hospitalized.
q. ______________________
r. ______________________
s. ______________________
t. ______________________

Age 10

Today

> Yahweh, you are a compassionate
> and loving God,
> slow to anger, always kind and
> faithful.
> (Psalm 86:15)

It *Still* Hurts

When you lose something of value or someone close, you experience many confusing feelings. When your loss is great, your feelings of sadness are also great. Everybody experiences grief or sadness when they lose something or someone of importance. Grieving a loss is normal. Grieving helps people express their loss and deal with it. If a loss is rather small, like the misplacement of a possession, grieving does not take a lot of time and attention. But if the loss is great, like the death of a loved one, grieving takes longer and is more deeply felt.

When you are grieving a loss, you may do the following things:

- feel angry at the person who left or who caused your loss
- feel angry with God for a while
- be upset—for a long time or only for a little while
- find it hard to believe that you actually lost someone or something
- put off talking about your loss
- wish you could do something to change the situation
- discover that on some days you feel really sad, such as on days that have special meaning
- slowly but surely feel better for longer periods of time
- find something or someone else to help fill the empty place you feel because of your loss

When you are grieving a loss, the best thing you can do is to talk to someone about it. Confide in an adult whom you trust. This person cannot give you back what is gone, but she or he might be able to help you handle your feelings.

I still miss those I loved who are no longer with me but I find I am grateful for having loved them. The gratitude has finally conquered the loss. (Rita Mae Brown)

REMEMBER *These Things*

When your friend is hurting, *do* things that can help:

- Say something; your friend needs to know that you care.
- Try to be a good listener.
- If you feel comfortable doing so, give your friend a hug.
- Expect your friend to be moody, even angry.
- Know that it takes a long time to get over some kinds of pain.
- If you sense that your friend is becoming extremely sad, and you are afraid that he or she does not want to live, seek help for your friend.

When your friend is hurting, *don't* do things that might harm:

- Don't avoid your friend.
- Don't pretend that nothing happened. Silence will not make your friend's pain go away.
- Don't say things that blame your friend or that make light of your friend's pain, such as, "You'll get over it," "Forget it," or "You're not the only one who has ever had problems."
- Don't offer words of sympathy that you do not feel.
- Don't assume that everything is all right if your friend is laughing and joking around all the time.

O Lord of wisdom and light,
we come to you broken and sad.
Those who have passed, leave without
saying good-bye,
which makes us very sad,
and sometimes even mad,
but I know you will help us get through this.
I ask for you to give me courage,
and take away my anger, Lord.
(Johnny Quintana, Green River, Wyoming)

Word of Hope and Care

"Blessed are those who mourn:
they shall be comforted."

(Matthew 5:5, NJB)

"I am the bread of life.
No one who comes to me
will ever hunger;
no one who believes in me will
ever thirst."

(John 6:35, NJB)

"If you make my word your home
you will indeed be my disciples;
you will come to know the truth, and
the truth will set you free."

(John 8:31–32, NJB)

For this is how God loved the
world: God gave Jesus to the
world, so that everyone who
has faith will not perish, but
will have eternal life.

(Adapted from
John 3:16)

"You are sad now,
but I shall see you again, and
your hearts will be full of joy,
and that joy no one shall take from
you."

(John 16:22, NJB)

"Peace I leave with you; my peace I
give to you. I do not give to you as
the world gives. Do not let your
hearts be troubled, and do not let
them be afraid."

(John 14:27, NRSV)

"Come to me, all of you who are weary
and carrying heavy burdens, and I will give
you rest. Take my yoke upon you, and learn
from me; for I am gentle and humble in heart,
and you will find rest for your soul. For my yoke
is easy, and my burden is light."

(Adapted from Matthew 11:28–30)

"Do not let your hearts
be troubled.
Believe in God,
believe also in me."

(John 14:1, NRSV)

REMEMBER *These Things*

- Everybody goes through different kinds of losses in their life. Even Jesus knew what it was like to have a friend die, to be rejected, and to be deserted by friends.
- As time goes by, things that were painful become easier to handle.
- Deeper losses take longer to adjust to. But even those who experience the pain of a great loss will survive.
- Friends and other loved ones can help by extending their care and concern. The love of others is the best healer.
- God knows each person's pain. In Jesus, God became one with humankind. Jesus experienced the joy and the pain of every person.

How Do I Spell Lonely?

Write your responses to these items in the spaces provided. The first three items are for your personal reflection. Be prepared to discuss your ideas about item 4.

1. Make a dot on the line below to indicate how often you feel lonely.

   I often feel lonely. ———————————— I almost never feel lonely.

2. Describe the last time you felt really lonely.

   7 years ago

3. List the three experiences that most make you feel lonely.

4. Identify the positive things you do to get over feelings of loneliness.

God,

I feel loneliness at school, between classes and at lunchtime. I feel depressed and lonely. I feel like I don't have many friends. When I am at home lying on my bed at night, I feel lonely. I feel depressed and sad whenever I get in a fight with my mom and dad. God, help me to always feel wanted and important. Help me to feel loved.

(D.A.S., a boy in Royal Oak, Michigan)

All by Myself

Write your responses to these items in the spaces provided. Be prepared to discuss your responses with your group.

1. Make a dot on the line below to indicate how often you choose to spend time alone.

   I often choose to be alone. ———————————— I never choose to be alone.

2. Make a dot on the line below to indicate how you feel about being alone.

   Being alone is fun. ———————————— Being alone bugs me.

Loneliness is the poverty of self; solitude is the richness of self. (May Sarton)

We have all known the long loneliness and we have learned that the only solution is love and that love comes with community. (Dorothy Day)

3. Describe the place you go to feel happy, quiet, and peaceful.
My moms room

4. List the things you like to do there.
Watch Youtube

5. Explain what you did the last time you were there.
Watched You tube

There are times
for doing nothing
but be sure you do it
well—
and listen.
For God, in silent
spaces,
has something great
to tell.
(Unknown)

REMEMBER *These Things*

- Being alone and being lonely are different experiences.
- Everyone is lonely sometimes.
- Loneliness can be painful, and we have to find ways to deal with it. Things like call-ing a friend, finding a hobby, and joining a team can help you deal with loneliness.
- All human beings need time alone without the usual distractions of life, in order to think, to dream, to regroup, and to just be themselves. Another word for aloneness like this is *solitude.*
- Try to spend at least a few minutes in solitude every day.

JOY Will Get You Through

Read the sections below, and take some time to reflect on them quietly and to complete the sentence-starters.

J Is for "Jesus"

"Come to me, all you who labor and are burdened, and I will give you rest." (Matthew 11:28, NAB)

No matter what happens, Jesus knows what you are going through. Remember that Jesus had the same kinds of happy and sad times that you have. In knowing Jesus you can understand how much God wants happiness for you. Take time to talk to God. Remember that God knows what you need even before you ask, but God likes to hear from you. Trust God, and know that nothing is too small for God to care about, and nothing is too big for God to handle.

One really great thing that God has done for me is

____

When I think about my relationship to God, I think that I will

____

O Is for "Others"

The LORD God said: "It is not good for the man to be alone. I will make a suitable partner for him." (Genesis 2:18, NAB)

God created Eve to be a friend and a companion to Adam. This was God's way of telling us that God wants people to be companions and friends. Friends and family get you over bumps when you are upset. You need them, and you were made to have them. Friends and family need you too.

The next time I am going through a tough time, I am going to talk to this person:

____

I am going to help someone else by

____

Y Is for "Yourself"

You are created in God's own image, and you are wonderful in God's eyes. God does not make mistakes. Believe in yourself. Take charge of your own life.

I give you thanks that I am wonderfully made; wonderful are your works. *(Adapted from Psalm 139:14)*

I really did a good job of handling a tough time when I

___

The next time I am involved in a tough situation, I know I can

___

REMEMBER *These Things*

- Know that tough times do not last forever.
- Find positive ways to deal with your stress.
- Rely on God, other people, and your inner strength to get you through life's struggles.
- Always have hope.

Dear God,

As odd as it may seem, I thank You for the troubles in my life. It was the hard times in my life that I learned from the most. From these times I learned courage, strength, and most of all that when it seems that everything in my life has failed, I can turn to You. It was when my head was down and my heart was aching that I was truly able to see God in my life. I saw You in my sister's sweet smile and in my mother's gentle touch that told me that one day, maybe not today or tomorrow, but one day it would be okay. You were with me every step of the way, and now it is okay. Lord, it is the trouble and misfortune in my life that has allowed me to truly appreciate the happiness You have placed in my life.

(Victoria McCardell, Lafayette, Louisiana)

My Letter to God

Use these sentence-starters to write your personal letter to God. Trust that God truly is interested in you and your thoughts. God really wants to hear from you.

Dear God,

Our group has talked about a lot of stuff when it has been together. I have really thought hard about

I need your help with this one, God. The tough time that is bothering me the most right now is

I am going to try to

I know that life is not all bad, God. A lot of good things happen in my life too. Here are some of the good things:

Before I say good-bye, I just want to tell you

Love,

Always be joyful, then, in the Lord; I repeat, be joyful. Let your good sense be obvious to everybody. The Lord is near. Never worry about anything; but tell God all your desires of every kind in prayer and petition shot through with gratitude, and the peace of God which is beyond our understanding will guard your hearts and your thoughts in Christ Jesus. (Philippians 4:4–7, NJB).